THE HEALTH SERVICE:
PAST, PRESENT AND FUTURE

UNIVERSITY OF LONDON
HEATH CLARK LECTURES *1973*
delivered at
The London School of Hygiene and Tropical Medicine

The Health Service:
Past, Present and Future

by

SIR GEORGE GODBER

G.C.B., D.M., F.R.C.P., F.F.C.M., D.P.H.

Former Chief Medical Officer,
Department of Health and Social Security

UNIVERSITY OF LONDON
THE ATHLONE PRESS
1975

Published by
THE ATHLONE PRESS
UNIVERSITY OF LONDON
at 4 Gower Street, London WC1

Distributed by
Tiptree Book Services Ltd
Tiptree, Essex

U.S.A. and Canada
Humanities Press Inc
New York

© *University of London* 1975

ISBN 0 485 26324 6

Printed in Great Britain by
WESTERN PRINTING SERVICES LTD
BRISTOL

PREFACE

I was greatly honoured by the University of London in their invitation to give the Heath Clark Lectures for 1973 at the London School of Hygiene and Tropical Medicine, my own old School of Public Health. I have heard many Heath Clark Lectures, starting with those of 1936 with the then Dean and my former Chief, the late Sir Wilson Jameson, in the Chair. It was not in my mind then and has not been since that I might myself be given the honour of delivering the lectures.

Since the National Health Service is my subject it may well be thought that two lectures would hardly be sufficient but I do not propose to give an exhaustive account of the Health Service as a whole—that requires a larger book. In the first lecture I propose to deal with the origin and inception of the Health Service and in the second with progress and prospects, but I do not intend to become deeply involved with administrative performance or concepts either of the past or of the future except in so far as they relate directly to standards of care. I apologise in advance for an account which is, of necessity, episodic and incomplete.

CONTENTS

I

THE ORIGIN AND INCEPTION
OF THE HEALTH SERVICE

An understanding of any health service requires more than an account of a structure at any one time. There have been examples of services virtually created anew, but in most countries the organization of health care—by that I mean the care provided by the medical profession and those others who work with it—evolves over a long period of time. Some of the components of a service derive their shape from the form of local government or of the administration of other social services which contribute to the health of the public. The USSR in 1918, Yugoslavia in 1945 and the Peoples' Republic of China in 1947 had to face universities which had been destroyed, medical schools which had been dispersed and the absence of a tradition of medical services that reached all the people. They could only deal with their situation by an immediate intensified production of doctors through newly created medical schools, using such staff as remained to them and preparing their teachers anew. Having begun to produce doctors for the health services, they had to ensure a reasonable distribution throughout their countries of trained staff which they knew would be inadequate in numbers for many years. The USSR developed the *feldsher* and China the barefoot doctor to provide immediate help. They were faced with great problems in controlling communicable disease and they could only hope to handle these through standardized procedures centrally defined. They had to do on an enormous scale the sort of thing that military forces would have to do in order to provide for their own peculiar requirements and they succeeded in doing it to an extent which is far too little appreciated in this country. The result is in a regulated idiom that would be unacceptable in this country; that does not mean that it should be any less regarded in theirs.

A colonial service on the other hand would begin with the need to provide care for occupying forces and governing staff. In a developing country with its own peculiar problems of communicable disease there would immediately be problems of controlling such diseases in the community in order to prevent their transmission to occupying forces. From that starting point some limited service could be extended outward. Countries being populated by immigrant European stock tended to establish services, or a lack of them, originally paralleling those of the home country and only to diverge from them with the evolution of different customs. In New Zealand, for instance, elected Hospital Boards with substantial Central Government finance date from the latter part of the nineteenth century. There the distinction between specialties and general practice was emerging when their service began in 1940 but specialties are not yet so differentiated as in Britain because their system encourages it less. In Australia, the tradition of unpaid service in voluntary hospitals remained as it did in Britain until 1948, but Canada followed the pattern of the United States where patients paid for their own medical care in hospital. In Brazil, a single charitable organization inherited from Portugal established a chain of voluntary hospitals later to be supplemented by state and insurance based hospitals. In Sweden and Denmark, on the other hand, a far more orderly pattern of development occurred from the middle of the last century, related to prepayment insurance systems, with county authorities responsible for the provision of general hospital services and therefore of most of the specialties. Thus there were recognized and accepted overall controlling health authorities long before local government was playing a real part in the provision of organized medical care in Britain. An area hospital authority which could grow naturally into an area health authority had the confidence of the public and the professions alike, but such a confidence was not to be found anywhere in Britain at that time. Even in Sweden, until quite recently, some services remained outside the local administration—mental hospitals being centrally financed by the Ministry of Social Affairs under the guidance of the Royal Medical Board. Teaching hospitals in Denmark were controlled by the

Ministry of Education rather than the National Health Service, whose ministerial authority was the Ministry of Social Affairs. But there was in both countries acceptance of a duty on Central and Local Government working together and supported by insurance schemes to provide an overall system of health care even though its administration was radically modified at a later stage. There were arrangements under which token fees were paid by the patient to the doctor, but there was not the kind of insistence, which existed in Britain up until 1948, on the right of the profession to charge private fees to all those outside the lower income groups. This was an important factor in securing earlier and more complete acceptance in these Scandinavian countries of organization of the provision of medical care. In Britain the tradition that specialists provided unpaid service in voluntary hospitals meant that the major medical institutions could not become instruments of direct medical profit as they could in North America. The absence of fee per service payments to hospital medical staff in Britain also prevents the system of extra-hospital consultation with specialists which presents such difficulties in the organization of hospital care and the development of medical teaching in Australia and the Federal Republic of Germany.

I have deliberately devoted my opening paragraphs to the discussion of other health services than our own in order to illustrate some of the ways in which traditional approaches can affect not only the way in which an organized health service is eventually fitted together but also the efficiency of its development. The crucial step is from the proposition that all the population should be empowered to buy medical care in the market to that of the national responsibility to provide an integrated service through health professions which cease to rely on individual fees as their main source of income. The turning point is in fact in Section 1 of the National Health Service Act 1946. 'It shall be the duty of the Minister of Health to secure the provision of health services for the population of England and Wales.' As I said earlier, that provision in the 1946 Act is not the start of health services in Britain. It is the turning point where the country moves from a mixture of private and gap-filling public services to a system of care which sets out to meet all needs in so far as they can be met. Naturally, the way in which those services were to be put together in 1948 depended upon what existed before 5 July 1948.

Until the middle of the nineteenth century there were no services in any really organized sense, but there were one or two contributions. There had been some private ventures like that of Dr Lettsom in the eighteenth century, running a sort of doctor's club or private panel system amongst the well-to-do in return for an annual retention fee. Perhaps the direct ancestors were the doctors' clubs which existed in urban and even in rural areas until the end of the nineteenth century and still for mothers and children up to the time of the inception of the National Health Service. The Friendly Societies had the object of providing money payments to employed members during sickness and contracted with doctors to provide medical care, but dependents were only included in a few industrial schemes like that of the Great Western Railway. There were charitably organized poor people's dispensaries, often linked with hospitals, in some of our larger cities to fill some of the gaps. The Great Western Railway Welfare Society in 1948 actually handed over a substantial health centre building and a small hospital in Swindon. In some of the mining areas in particular there were quite well found hospitals often with some kind of specialist staff provided by Friendly Societies which paid salary or capitation fees to doctors who undertook general practice in the same areas. Particularly in South Wales there were populations which would not have had any local hospital services but for such provision as this. I recall one 40-bed hospital in south Yorkshire which was in effect the service for one colliery complex and the villages where the miners lived.

The Friendly Societies and doctors' clubs had one important effect; they did secure location of medical practitioners within reach of the whole population. The payments they made were commonly small and, in areas where doctors were wholly dependent on such payments, the ratio of population to doctors was far too large. In rural areas there could be other factors. For instance one such practice known to me is still located in a house provided in the middle of the nineteenth century by the owner of the nearby mansion so that there should be an apothecary at his gate and incidentally able to provide service on horseback to a group of villages in a radius of some six miles. There were probably enough fee-paying patients in such an area to make the practice a good deal more lucrative and attractive than that in a mining valley. It is interesting to note that in Australia the large number of individual insurance schemes still include some which are not much larger than individual doctors' clubs.

The real point about this development was that it brought medical attention physically within reach, but not necessarily economically so. When National Health Insurance for employed workers came in 1911, the system received the important stabilizing and supporting influence of a nationally organized insurance system and provided one main component from which the National Health Service was to develop in 1948. Whatever may be said about greater development of and expenditure on hospitals in the last 25 years, it was general practice, sustained for 37 years by National Health Insurance and gaining substantial additional support from the new system, which really carried the National Health Service at its inception.

The hospital services developed from widely differing origins. There were monastery infirmaries from very early times, a handful of which continued after the dissolution of the monasteries with other support of a voluntary nature, and there were some lazar houses for the segregation of the infected, few of which survived the dissolution. The earliest foundations of voluntary hospitals, apart from these survivals, took place in the middle of the eighteenth century when such as Guy's Hospital and some of the major County Infirmaries, including the Radcliffe Infirmary at Oxford and the Norfolk and Norwich Hospital, first appeared. Within one hundred years a large number of such hospitals or infirmaries was established and around about the middle of the nineteenth century there also appeared special hospitals for children and for women. Such establishments as the Royal Manchester Children's Hospital, the Children's Hospital in Birmingham and the Jessop Hospital for Women in Sheffield date from this time. But although these hospitals, established by charities, were to be the main foci for the development of medical education and of specialist services for a century, there were other developments of equal significance for the National Health Service of the future, when it had to assume the responsibility of comprehensive hospital care for the population. There had been some smallpox hospitals of a primitive kind in London before the end of the eighteenth century. Isolation hospitals were to emerge later as hospitals for smallpox and for infectious disease provided as a duty by local authorities. The Poor Law Act of 1835 led to the widespread development of institutions, which included infirmaries only because medical indigence could be a reason for admission to, and retention in, such an institution. These institutions and hospitals for the mentally ill and retarded were to provide over two-thirds of the accommodation taken over by the National Health Service in 1948 and there were later added hospitals for tuberculosis. Less than a quarter of usable hospital beds taken over by the National Health Service in 1948 were in voluntary hospitals.

The Poor Law infirmaries and hospitals for the mentally ill were primarily intended to serve a custodial function, and even hospitals for infectious disease were originally for isolation. The name of the agency which provided institutions in London, 'The Metropolitan Asylums Board' which was to last until 1929, is an indication of the functions local authorities were expected to fulfil. Since the object was custodial, the institutions were isolated and often walled and many of the county mental hospitals were deep in the country. It was common to find city hospitals built on cheap peripheral sites near other facilities like the refuse disposal works and sewage disposal plant. 'Boundary House' was a name often given to the Poor Law Infirmary because that was what it was. People went to those institutions to stay there and the continuity with their real lives which visiting could provide was hardly recognized at all. It could be economical to provide wards in the infirmary block of a general institution to accommodate those with mental handicap or senile dementia. Some of those units were later to be refurbished and become the first of our psychiatric units in general hospitals under the Manchester Regional Hospital Board. Nevertheless, towards the end of the nineteenth century and during the phase of hospital building before the First World War, substantial hospital units with improved, though still Nightingale-type, wards were provided on a considerable scale. Some, like the Derby City Hospital or the Broad Green Hospital, Liverpool, were designed as separate general units, although on land adjoining the rest of the institution and commonly sharing some services with it. It was in these hospitals more than in voluntary hospitals that extra provision to meet casualty requirements of the Second World War was made.

Neither the Poor Law infirmaries nor the voluntary hospitals, in the main, had facilities for isolation of communicable disease. The emergence of preventive medicine in the middle of the nineteenth century led to the establishment of hospitals for communicable disease. The 1875 Public Health Act put upon local authorities, that is local District Councils, the responsibility of providing for the control of communicable disease and that meant isolation of patients and, almost incidentally, treatment of the patient in isolation. The fact that this responsibility rested upon District Councils and that horse-drawn transport limited the distance of removal of patients, led to the establishment of many small isolation units which were manifestly inefficient as soon as treatment had been discovered and means of transport over considerable distances evolved. There were a very few voluntary hospitals that provided for communicable disease, for instance the Stamford and Rutland General Infirmary and the London Fever Hospital. Very often provision was made in rural districts by the conversion of some isolated house, or, in urban districts, in buildings sometimes adjoining the sewage farms. Separate provision was always made for smallpox.

As a very early example of central hospital planning, model plans for small infectious disease units were produced by the Local Government Board and such buildings still exist with provision within one single floor block for diphtheria, scarlet fever and typhoid, so arranged that isolation is secured by having access between the wings housing different diseases only through the ward kitchen. So firmly do some of these small hospitals become entrenched that many of them were still in use in 1948, although long outdated and unsuitable for modern treatment. It is interesting to recall that even as recently as thirty years ago the Ministry of Health was thinking in terms of one bed per 1000 of the population for the reception of patients with communicable disease. We do not use one bed per 10 000 now and there is not a single hospital left in England solely for the reception of notifiable disease except for some smallpox hospitals on a care and maintenance basis.

Separate hospital units for the treatment of pulmonary tuberculosis began to appear at the beginning of this century, apart from a few places like the Brompton Hospital which had existed earlier. Dispensary services appeared at about the same time, usually as completely separate out-patient departments which were later to acquire their own radiological facilities. The 1911 National Health Insurance Act provided for sanatorium benefit until the power of local authorities to provide a tuberculosis service became a duty. Some local authorities, County or City Councils, discharged that responsibility by adapting and extending disused mansion houses, bought in the first twenty years of the century. Some, having to meet urgent needs at short notice, had hutted hospitals erected with little or no provision for heating because exposure was then thought to be an essential part of the treatment. Some of those old sanatoria had been on bleak hill tops with open-sided wards from which the drifted snow might literally have to be shovelled before the patients could be reached in the morning. Many had been modernized, but even in the middle 1930s the Nuffield Orthopaedic Centre at Oxford had otherwise well-planned new wards provided without central heating. Nevertheless, the group of beds for tuberculosis provided about five per cent of the total taken over in 1948, and some sanatoria had developed well-built active units usable for other purposes, sadly all too often in the wrong place.

It is difficult for the present generation of doctors to appreciate how much effort went into tuberculosis services even 35 years ago. They were a major preoccupation of local health authorities and there were 20 000 deaths and nearly 30 million days lost from work as a result of tuberculosis only a little over twenty years ago. Indeed I can recall at that time going to South Wales to try to persuade the chest physicians there to take part in pneumoconiosis panel work and being rejected because they were convinced that they would continue to be fully occupied with pulmonary tuberculosis today.

From 1920 onwards, local authorities had also had responsibility for providing maternity services, but as recently as 1938 the majority of confinements were still taking place at home, even in London. Local authority maternity units were often separate and too small, or were converted blocks in what had been Poor Law infirmaries. Only a minority were purpose-built and well designed. Evacuation from the cities during the last war strangely enough provided the impetus which led women in rural as well as urban areas to seek hospital delivery, because in many rural areas maternity homes for the evacuees were established in large converted houses.

The administration of health services was through a highly confused pattern of different administrations. The Metropolitan Asylums Board for the area of the London County, later taken over by the LCC Health Department, is one of the few examples of co-ordination in the local authority field. There was a single tuberculosis service in Wales, with centralized sanatoria. There were some Joint Committees or Boards for providing mental hospitals. There were some combinations for providing infectious disease hospitals. But within a large local authority there could be several different agencies, not primarily concerned with health, responsible for the different pieces of a hospital service. In a single county there could be several small independent hospitals for infectious disease under District Councils or Joint Boards, separate mental services, several independent MCW (Maternity and Child Welfare) authorities, hospitals in parts of Public Assistance Institutions under a separate committee which also provided a District doctor for the indigent, a dozen voluntary hospitals, a county nursing association, volunteer and police ambulances, a treatment scheme under the Cancer Act, and Tuberculosis and VD Services, each self-contained. The Local Government Act of

1929 was intended to bring some order into this confusion and gave authorities an option, not used by all, to transfer health responsibilities from Public Assistance Committees, which took over the Poor Law, to the Public Health Committees. In some areas this had begun to lead to separation of hospital from purely custodial functions, but the nature of some of the old complicated institutions made this extremely difficult. A line might be drawn between the public assistance or social welfare section and the hospital section of a large mixed institution which perhaps left boilers and the laundry to the public assistance side and the kitchen to the public health or hospital side. In one county there was almost open warfare between public health and public assistance over the disposition of the pigsties in one particular institution. Sometimes a hospital which was appropriated to public health left with public assistance the wards for the chronic sick. But in some areas as in the Parts of Lindsey, Lincolnshire, a progressive hospital policy led to the building of new hospitals and maternity homes under public health according to the best concepts of the day, but unhappily not in accordance with the District General Hospital policy which was to emerge twenty-five years later. Still it was an advance: if only a short step in practice it was a long one in principle.

The third major component in the health service, also on the local authority side, was preventive personal health services provided mainly in clinics, but not including at that stage school health service. The maternity and child welfare services originated in a situation at the beginning of this century where proper care of the expectant mother for herself and her baby up to the confinement hardly existed at all. The registration and control of midwives which was introduced in 1905 was only a very short first step. On reading the first rules of the new Central Midwives Board for practising midwives, you will see all too clearly how primitive the practice of midwifery then was. Medical aid was to be called to a patient who was 'a dwarf or deformed' or had 'genital sores' or a 'discharge' or 'unduly prolonged labour'. The help that a midwife might get from any doctor at that time would depend on his experience, but there was virtually no provision for antenatal care. Still it was a beginning and maternity and child welfare clinics began to appear on a considerable scale where authorities chose before they had a duty, to make the first provision of organized care for mothers and children. Many of the clinics developed first under voluntary auspices often facing considerable hostility from doctors in the same area who thought that the object of clinics was to take work from them. In fact, the clinics were doing work which was otherwise not done at all. Gradually local authorities, some of them small Borough Councils, others powerful counties or county boroughs, developed this service generally as they were obliged to do after the Maternity and Child Welfare Act of 1919.

The clinics certainly were resented by general practitioners, though they must have generated a good deal of additional remunerative work for they did not try to treat but only to advise and refer where necessary for treatment. They often acted as if they were the antenatal out-patient departments of maternity units which were run by the same authority or by the county authority, though separately staffed and with different records. They were much criticized because doctors working at antenatal clinics were not doing midwifery in the sense of attending confinements. It had still not yet penetrated the minds of many general practitioners and even some obstetricians that safety in midwifery depends more upon meticulous antenatal care, provided it is in close communication with those who conduct the deliveries, than the mechanics of good obstetrics at delivery. During the thirty years before the Health Service began there was great improvement in the health of pre-school children not only because of the educational work done in the clinics that many doctors affected to despise, but also of the work that some of the doctors interested in children began to do for themselves and have since greatly extended under the Health Service. Some of this work was probably done in a perfunctory way and much of it was authoritarian more or less in accord with the ritual originally developed in New Zealand by Sir Henry Truby King. But it demonstrated the kind of change in infant care we needed and the improvements we are still obtaining may well arise in part from the fact that the young mothers of today, and even better the third generation mothers, have been able to learn rational child care from their own mothers and to use the services better.

In this work the most important component was probably non-medical. The health visitor, a nurse trained in preventive work and especially in baby care, could visit the homes routinely and not simply on request as a family doctor had to do. The request might never go to the doctor who, after all, had to be paid. The nurse, as her counterpart in Scandinavia had done, became an adviser to the mother perhaps at times a great deal closer to many of the problems of the young women than any clinic doctor is likely to be. Paediatrics through much of this period was differentiated from general medicine in a minority of hospitals. Even in a city of the size of Nottingham, there was no doctor practising only in paediatrics until the middle 1940s and the first whole-time paediatrician was appointed to the Sheffield Teaching Hospital only in 1946.

The number of clinics increased and health visiting services became universal, penetrating into every street of the city and to every village of the county. Even households too remote for the mother to reach a clinic could be reached by the health visitor. Periodically the mother could be taken to the clinic and most of them were. Infant feeding must have been revolutionized over a period of twenty years. Rickets was largely eliminated and infant mortality halved. However, despite an increase in antenatal care, no real impact was made on maternal mortality until the introduction of the first anti-bacterial drugs. By 1936 there was provision for domiciliary visits by specialists in cases of obstetric difficulty and there was even the beginning of a home help service. Because local authority hospitals provided most of the maternity beds, the clinic preventive services and the hospital services were beginning to come closer together. General practice still remained splendidly (perhaps it should be ingloriously) isolated, but there were even beginning to be inter-hospital linkages. The teaching hospitals of Birmingham had come together, the Sheffield Royal Infirmary and Royal Hospital had a concordat if not a real unity. The professorial obstetric unit in Bristol and a professorial paediatric unit in Newcastle were in city hospitals not in the voluntary teaching hospital.

The Nuffield Trust, as it then was, sponsored a survey of hospital services in Berkshire, Buckinghamshire and Oxfordshire. The 1933 Local Government Act had made possible the establishment of Joint Hospital Planning Councils, though few paid more than lip-service to the idea of district planning. The Cancer Act of 1939 provided for local authority schemes to secure facilities for the treatment of cancer, particularly by radiotherapy. One such scheme in Lincolnshire actually came to fruition with the opening of a new radiotherapy centre at Scunthorpe during the war. A Radium Commission was established to help provide radiation sources.

Finally came the war and with it the necessity of a scheme for dealing with casualties both from air-raids and from illness in sections of the population that had been evacuated from the cities. A complete survey had been undertaken of all hospitals of whatever kind and many other buildings were earmarked for auxiliary hospitals. It was estimated that 550 000 beds could be provided for casualties within the first month; a fanciful estimate indeed, but, none the less, large provision was made and many hospitals were provided with additional facilities for surgical treatment and for investigation, some with additional beds in hutted wards. A nationwide system was organized, guided by Regional Hospital Officers appointed by the Department or Sector Officers based on London and plans were made, and put into effect when war broke out, for hospitals from city centres to be evacuated to safer areas where sometimes a quality of service entirely new to the area was thus provided.

The emergency medical service operated at once when war began. Within a year it was dealing not merely with the sick amongst the evacuees but also with large numbers of casualties from air-raids and the Forces and with the acutely ill who had to be sent out from the centre of the cities. Local authority health departments were the local agents for much of this and by the time the system had coped with casualties evacuated from Europe, or a large part of them, it had been shown that the hospital service, at least, could be organized outside the large cities. In order to give the service needed, special units of many kinds had to be established and diagnostic services radically improved.

These were changes that authorities and administrations of various kinds had brought about. They could not have been achieved if the professions had not been prepared for change. The first major indication of medical readiness for change had been the report of an Advisory Committee chaired by Lord Dawson, reporting in 1921 on the form of a future health service for the nation. That report was written essentially in terms of using and supporting existing services. It is credited with the original idea of the health centre, but it was concerned more with institutions and their staffing than with necessary changes in the organization of medical practice, except for the clear indication of the need for concentration. The BMA (British Medical Association) early in the 1939–45 War set up its own Medical Planning Commission. An independent younger group, called Medical Planning Research, also prepared proposals. It is not worth examining in detail the nature of the administrations proposed, but the essence of the reports of both groups was that the majority of the population needed organized provision of health care. The new element was recognition that neither the profession nor the public could really go it alone in future. An organization was necessary to plan and support the provision of the range and quality of services the public need.

Lord Beveridge in his report on social security assumed that a National Health Service would be provided, and further that provision of such a service would lead to improvements in health and reduce absence from work through sickness. He missed the point that better health, if it led to longer life, inevitably led during that longer life to a greater use of services. The Beveridge report was followed by the 1944 White Paper which analysed the nature of the services we had and the need for the future, but still envisaged provision of comprehensive services through arrangements made with the kind of agencies that already existed. It contemplated some concentration and it foresaw the need for regional planning, but it did not propose the radical changes that were subsequently judged necessary, including particularly the transfer of ownership of hospitals.

Meanwhile the Nuffield Trust had continued its work on the development of regional systems for hospital provision and in collaboration with the health departments had arranged for teams of surveyors, usually two doctors and one administrator, to examine the hospitals in each region and to make recommendations for their future. That series of reports has largely been forgotten, but it did provide much of the basic information upon which the Regional Hospital Boards had to work in 1947 and 1948. The surveys did not extend to the hospitals for the mentally ill or handicapped which were still treated as if they were an entirely separate problem, and administered by special local authority committees supervised centrally by the Board of Control, which was outside the Ministry of Health proper. The common theme of all those survey reports is that, district by district, the hospitals must be brought together, to be run as district services. At that time there might be half a dozen or more entirely separate administrations responsible for pieces of the hospital service which are now (1973) under a single Hospital Management Committee. The management of personal preventive services might be separate again and general practice was completely independent. There could be no doubt of the need for concentration, the question only was how far that concentration should go. Some argued for a health authority which would simply contract with the existing authorities to provide the services they already provided. Such a system would have involved little immediate disturbance and would have provided funds without which voluntary hospitals would shortly have been bankrupt, but it would have led to endless duplication of work and opportunity for confusion. It would have made coherent planning almost impossible; the difficulties could be partially overcome, as they have been in Canada, but only by an outlay we could not afford.

No-one thought general practice would do other than continue on the lines on which it was already established, although there was much talk of health centres. The only real argument was whether it was to be a service available to 100 per cent of the people or whether there was to be some cut-off point based on income and above which there would be no entitlement to those patients who paid privately. The preventive services were already with the local authorities which had developed them and there was no early prospect of local government reform which waited twenty years for London and is only now being achieved for the rest of the country. The personal preventive services could be transferred from the largest district councils which had maternity and child welfare powers to Counties and increased participation of general practitioners could be encouraged, but despite much trumpeting about the importance of preventive medicine there was little coherent thought about what it might do. Some services, like home nursing and ambulances, clearly had to be reorganized and supported and new possibilities were foreseen for after-care and home help but most thinking was in terms of more use of old methods. We were then in the last months of the war and the so-called Caretaker Coalition Government had to begin the discussions following on the White Paper with the professions, the British Hospital Association, representing voluntary hospitals, and the local authorities. It all had a slightly unreal air until the General Election of 1945 had made it clear what Government was to be responsible for the formulation and inception of the reforms. There was no doubt that a comprehensive service must come, only doubt of its form. We were still not very far away from the approach of Australia except that the new health service was to be based upon central government funds and not upon insurance.

Two vital decisions were taken by the new Government at the instance of Aneurin Bevan. It was decided that the ownership of all the public hospitals, whether they were owned by local authorities or voluntary bodies, was to be transferred to the Minister of Health. The hospitals so transferred were to be administered by Regional Hospital Boards, working through Hospital Management Committees. The Boards were to be appointed, not elected, and they in turn were to appoint the Committees. That decision was, to my mind, the vital one for the future of the Health Service. It made possible district planning by a regional authority and rational staffing controlled by a regional authority, with assessment of the quality of applicants for specialist posts by properly appointed specialist

Advisory Committees which could guard against local favouritism on the one hand and favouritism from the academic centres on the other. Without this organizational approach we would still be a very long way from the possibility of unification that we now have before us in 1974 and I believe that a revision of the National Health Service Act would have been required very much earlier. Without it the direct contribution of the 1950s, which was the development of a properly planned specialist staff, and of the 1960s, which was physical concentration for efficiency and redeployment on the basis of District General Hospitals, could not have been achieved. The second vital decision was that the service should be open to all on the basis of medical need, allowing private treatment for those patients who wished to use it, but giving no technical advantage to patient or practitioner as a result. These two decisions distinguish the British from many other developed health services and they simplify the planning approach while assuming the burden of generalization of all services which has grown so much more onerous. A service of benefit to one patient must now be made available to all who need it and it is that which now sometimes extends us beyond our capacity and demands decisions on priorities which no-one had to make before.

In effect the approach to the reorganization was first to change the organization of hospital services on a basis which gave prospects of rapid redevelopment of specialist services, second a holding operation on general medical and dental practice, one which brought in the whole population, and assumed that the independent contractor relationship which would continue was still compatible with the orderly development of general practice, even if it became based on health centres, and third to link general practice more closely with the local authority preventive services and give both treatment branches the support they needed from other community services. The pharmaceutical and ophthalmic services were of course essential partners of general medical and dental practice in a comprehensive service. The local health authorities were to lose in total a far larger stake in hospital ownership and management than the voluntary bodies had collectively possessed, but they were to plan and develop community services more coherently and extensively than before.

I do not propose to talk about the negotiations, open and surreptitious, which preceded the inception of the Service on 5 July 1948. There were histrionics on both sides, there were withdrawals and accusations of bad faith; but in the end with what now seem trivial concessions the profession was persuaded to drop its intransigent attitude on what were, after all, not major questions and it was agreed to establish the Health Service substantially as it had been planned. One factor had caused more difficulty than any other, the insistence of the profession on being paid for general practice services solely on a capitation basis, paid out of a central pool. It seems odd that so few years later we should have come almost to another breakdown in order to get rid of the central pool. An attempt to introduce a part salary payment system, which would have made the handling of the expenses element, for example, very much easier, was so much anathema to the profession that an Amending Act had to be introduced, undertaking that a salaried system in general practice would not be introduced under the National Health Service Act. The odd sequel to that is that part of the settlement of general practitioner remuneration in 1966 involved a 'basic practice allowance'. Yet the profession's reaction was not purely selfish; it reflects the unease which understandably existed at the possibility of invasion of genuine, not merely financial, professional freedom. Even the financial implications were cause for justifiable concern in 1948 as the outcome of the adjudication on general practice earnings was to confirm four years later.

To some of us as we face the reorganization in 1974 it may seem odd that unification of administration was not insisted upon in 1948. It is my personal view that it would have been completely impossible to insist on such a thing at that time. We had little enough experience of hospital administration and none on a district or regional basis. The only units upon which we could at that time have concentrated the administration of all the Health Service would have been local authorities. The local authorities then had boundaries which were quite inappropriate for health service administration, dividing

County Borough from County and using areas that might have been quite appropriate for recruiting the Saxon fyrd a thousand years ago, but are almost wholly irrelevant to the needs of health services now. By leaving with rate-financed bodies only those services which could largely be organized on local government areas, any problem of cross-payment between authorities for services was avoided. By setting up entirely new authorities to do the entirely new job of regional planning and district administration of hospital services, we gave ourselves a chance to bring about a radical reorganization in that sector of the Health Service which was at the point of collapse in the absence of Government financial support. In the intervening twenty-five years many people have learned a great deal about the needs and organization of health services which in any area are now divided only between three authorities, some of which have cross-membership with the others. We are already thinking in district terms on many things. District organization of hospitals, district organization of postgraduate medical education, district links between general practice and hospitals, and full integration of the specialist services. We already know the benefits we can get from regional planning and organization of hospital medical manpower and perhaps some of its limitations. It was difficult enough to get the necessary organization on the hospital side introduced within a period of two years. The Appointed Day originally decided upon had to be postponed by three months. Had the reorganization been any more far-reaching, I believe it would have been thought unacceptable, especially by general practitioners, and unless it had been under local authorities it could not have been done. Moreover a regional tier was essential and there was none in local government. Since the local authorities were inappropriately shaped and unacceptable to the professions, I believe the 1946 Act went as far as it could.

The greatest problem at the inception was to get the new hospital organization on its feet. The first meeting of a Regional Hospital Board occurred in Sheffield at the beginning of July 1947. Few Regional Hospital Boards had more than a clerk or two in post before September. New staff had to learn the hospitals of their regions during the winter of 1947/48. They had to produce schemes for management groupings of their hospitals for approval by the Department before Hospital Management Committees could be appointed. A decision had to be made about the hospitals which were to be included in teaching groups and about the proprietary hospitals which were to be disclaimed and not transferred to the ownership of the Minister. Even on the basis that initially the new authorities would simply run things in their present form, there were many preparatory steps to be taken. Merely identifying the position of hospital medical staff was a tremendous job. A few of the Regional Board staff were men who had detailed knowledge of their regions but some had virtually none. The build-up of staff in support was necessarily slow. Many had been in the Forces during the war and, in hospitals, many increases were needed in senior staff and could only be provided by temporary arrangements made under the Emergency Medical Services for the appointment of trained men who would otherwise have had nowhere to go. There was an extraordinary situation of a shortage of medical manpower but also unemployment of doctors.

Local health authorities had to produce schemes for a range of services with which they were partly familiar but which included ambulance services of which they had only war-time experience—except in some of the cities—home nursing and the new development, home help and after care. Their written schemes had to be submitted for the Minister's approval and Regional Hospital Boards had to be consulted about them. There was bitter outcry about the loss of their hospitals. There were senior Medical Officers of Health saying that the end of public health was at hand, quite unmindful of the tremendous opportunities they were about to have in the development of preventive and supporting services once the load of hospital administration was taken from their departments.

In general practice there were administrative details connected with the end of the old Insurance Committee and the Friendly Society System and introduction of a differently constructed Executive Council to be funded from the Department. These changes made little impact on general practice itself, except that local medical, dental, pharmaceutical and optical committees had to be established in order to provide their share of nominations to the Executive Councils. An attempt was made to bring about some of the clearly desirable combinations of Executive Councils, for instance Nottingham and Nottinghamshire, Devon and Exeter, Kent and Canterbury, and Leicester and Rutland, but only those four were achieved.

The main problem about general practice was whether the profession would agree to come in at all. Eventually on the basis of some firm assurances which removed one area of uncertainty and in the face of the clear intention of hospital staff to enter the new Health Service, the profession as a whole accepted. They had to do this so far as general practice was concerned without a settlement on remuneration which the profession considered fair. Two committees chaired by Sir Will Spens had considered separately the remuneration of general practitioners and hospital medical staff. The recommendations for general practitioners were on a 1939 basis with a correction to be applied for the change in values. That piece of indecision was to lead to embitterment in the profession and a wrangle that lasted until an adjudication in 1952 finally gave virtually the adjustment for which the doctors had been asking. By comparison hospital staffs had done well for themselves and had accepted the Spens recommendations along with the system of merit award payments which must be unique, apart from the parallel of New Zealand, and has caused so much controversy within the profession since.

Finally there was agreement obtained with difficulty, after arduous negotiations between the medical and optical professions and the Department, on a supplementary ophthalmic service which was then intended to provide for the prescription and dispensing of spectacles only until such time as hospital ophthalmic services were able to deal with the whole service. It may not have been entirely amicable, but at least an uneasy peace between the opticians and the ophthalmologists was evolved for the first time.

Regional Boards had had nearly a year to prepare for the assumption of their responsibilities, but in that time they had had to appoint their headquarters' staff, decide on their schemes for hospital groups and obtain the Minister's approval and then to appoint Management Committees who had to appoint their staff. Even the decision about the transfers of some ex-local authority institutions were in doubt because they were joint user institutions. Executive Councils were more directly the heirs of the former Insurance Committees but their constitution was new and they were concerned with the whole population and not just the insured. The local health authorities had greater continuity and the Medical Officer of Health remained, but even they had new responsibilities and were ceding others. The absorption of independent MCW authorities' duties was seldom difficult for counties, even in London, Middlesex and the Soke of Peterborough where the changes were most radical.

There were forebodings of chaos on the Appointed Day but in the event, on 5 July 1948 services were given to patients just as they had been during the previous week. That should not have surprised anyone, for a health service is not primarily an administrative machine but rather a great number of personal acts of care for the sick by professionals who do not wait first to find how they will be paid. The immediate change was that from that date the cost of services was being met from central funds in hospital and in general medical and dental practice and mainly from the rate fund for the rest. There have since been charges of varying degree, but the great majority of cost is still met from central funds. From that date it has not been necessary to consider whether or not the individual is entitled to a service that he needs, and only in certain respects for relatively small charges, for instance for dental treatment, to secure payment at the time of treatment. It is freedom from that particular consideration for most of the population of this country and for most of the professions involved which is the most satisfying thing about the Health Service.

There were miscalculations of course. I have referred to one of them, the rate of remuneration of general practitioners, which in the light of the subsequent adjudication was seen to be unfair and which almost certainly led to the slow level of recruitment in the first four years of the service. It meant that none of the changes in general practice, for which many had hoped, really began to appear until the middle 1950s. There were some immediate and large increases in demand. The most obvious was that for spectacles because such a service had not previously been available for the elderly and there must have been many people in those first two or three years who were able to see well enough to do fine work again. There were shortages of time, of lenses and of frames and a back-log that took over two years to clear. It was an unprecedented demand, and perhaps might have been better foreseen, but it arose from one of the real social gains of the Health Service. The provision of hearing aids was new and that too led to an enormous demand which could only be satisfied by stages.

There was an immediate increase in demand on general practice, perhaps as much as 12 per cent, but it did not continue to grow, it was absorbed by the section of the medical profession which gets too little credit for having carried the heat and burden of the day in those first few years. There was a tremendous demand for dentistry, but in fact not on the scale that would have occurred if everyone had sought the dental treatment he needed. It was handled by a tremendous increase in the work accomplished by dentists whose capacity was seen to be so much greater than estimated that they, like the opticians and the ophthalmologists, suffered an early reduction in their individual fees.

The changes that could begin without delay were in hospital medical staffing. But there had first to be a painful process, the grading of hospital staff, undertaken of course by their professional colleagues. There were some senior staff, held not to be of consultant status, who had to be placed in an intermediate grade that even now has not completely disappeared. This was to cause a controversy that lasted through the first fifteen years of the service and of which there still remains an unhappy residue. In 1948 only about one clinician in seven was a consultant and the estimate of the relative importance of the grade was perhaps unrealistically high. Now that the proportion is greater than one in five, and one in three of all doctors entering permanent clinical careers is a consultant, greater realism prevails.

There was a large and continuing increase in hospital

medical staff, especially in the registrar and senior registrar grades, even though the senior registrar posts might be unable to offer the training that a senior registrar should expect.

In general, however, the mood for the first year or two was euphoric. Apart from constant disagreement about remuneration in general medical and dental practice and the sequel to a miscalculation of sight testing fees, the health professions as a whole were reasonably content. There was a revision of methods of payment but little radical change in the service.

There was for the first time a properly organized ambulance service. Domiciliary consultations by specialists could be obtained where necessary in the patient's home. Home help service was introduced and grew as rapidly as staff could be found. General practice, apart from the remuneration, went on as it had been, but with considerable changes in relative prosperity. For most, private practice almost disappeared overnight and the small but remunerative practice with a large and demanding private element suddenly became much less remunerative. The public health departments of local health authorities began to realize that after all they had not come to the end of their road and there were new vistas ahead.

So in 1948 we had come to a beginning. The radical change in administration and finance had been achieved without any substantial failure to provide service on 5 July. There was an odd euphoria about what had been done and a tendency to pride ourselves on having the finest health service in the world, as some people said. We were about to learn how much more costly the service would prove to be than the estimates upon which it had been introduced—based as they had to be on the inadequate information available from thousands of independent sources. We had not really looked at the size of the capital investment essential to a proper development of either community or hospital services. Still less were we aware of the demands that the rapidly accelerating development of medical science would make on capital and revenue expenditure, while it increased equally rapidly the possibility of intervention by the service for prevention or cure. We were shortly to learn that the Chancellor of the Exchequer of the day set a maximum of £400 million to the expenditure of central funds on the service—a measure perhaps of the failure in all countries to appreciate how much the cost of good health care would increase.

2

NATIONAL HEALTH SERVICE— PROGRESS AND PROSPECTS IN MEDICAL CARE

We have seen how, on 5 July 1948 diverse elements had been brought together as one health service, albeit managed as three different components. But some health service elements— school and occupational health services—were left outside the National Health Service.

Medical research was mainly the concern of the Research Councils and the universities; medical education was mainly financed through the University Grants Committee and the administrative responsibility of the Boards of Governors was to provide facilities for medical education and research, not to undertake it.

The time was one of material shortages. With all the other capital reconstruction work required in the country, there was little to spare for hospitals. Funds, building materials, and labour for any health purpose were minimal. There were some war-time temporary hospitals in the right place, or near it, and capable of continued use at a cost. Often they had primitive facilities, lacking even the amenity of central heating. Almost none of the hospital development between the wars had been envisaged as the planning of a hospital service to meet the whole need of the population of a district. It may well have been a blessing in disguise that the capital available for the Health Service was so limited. Otherwise plans of the 1930s might have been taken out, dusted off and implemented instead of replacing them by the new regional and district planning the National Health Service now made possible. Some of the hospital building carried out in the United States under the Hill-Burton Act shows clearly the mistakes that can be made in capital development planned for the institution rather than overall public need. By contrast, despite the devastation of war, Finland made a good approach to hospital building with regional planned development on lines already adopted by other Scandinavian countries. The Health Service saddled with something like 3,600 hospitals largely old and defective in structure, and wrongly located, not only had to waste effort maintaining service with inefficient plant, but also had to spend what little capital there was making these bad old units usable for modern treatment. It says much for the devotion of hospital staff—especially nurses—that such good service was given.

Buildings, of course, are not the main factors in the quality of hospital care. Good staff can do good work in a barn. It was possible to regroup and expand available professional staff. The groupings of hospitals for management purposes brought together different hospital units serving the same population and made it possible to rationalize distribution of specialties and reorganize arrangements for training of nurses, technicians and junior doctors. Indifference, even antagonism had often existed between neighbouring units and this could gradually be overcome. For instance the Public Assistance Hospital, and the voluntary County Hospital in Bedford became jointly the Bedford General Hospital, North and South Wings; the specialties and nurses' training regrouped in the combined unit. What had been long-stay accommodation for the chronic mentally ill in the municipal institutions of some of the Lanca-shire county boroughs, was refurnished and became acute psychiatric units dealing with short-stay patients. Some of the old, small, redundant infectious disease hospitals and sanatoria could become annexes of various kinds or be discarded and closed down. These things could be done because medical and nursing staff in each group had one employer.

The Service could and did recruit immediately to new specialist posts, doctors trained in the Forces during the war. In many provincial centres well-trained and experienced specialists who formerly had to supplement earnings as specialists in general practice could now turn wholly to the specialist side of their work. The result of all this was an

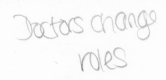

immediate and large increase in the amount of specialist time available, especially in hospital centres outside the large cities. By the end of 1949 there had been a substantial increase and the equivalent of the whole-time three and a half thousand consultants was provided by the five and a half thousand individuals available in England and Wales. This process was to continue and by the end of 1970 there were two and a half times as much consultant time and double the number of medical staff in all grades. In the same period the number of nursing staff including the number of trained nurses doubled; the hospital professional and technical staff, other than doctors and nurses, increased more than two and a half times and included many new technologies and skills.

The group of professions supplementary to medicine was reorganized on lines recommended by a committee chaired by Sir Zachary Cope. Provision was made for their registration and regulation and a General Optical Council was also set up.

General medicine and general surgery were the largest medical specialties in 1948 but increased little after the first few years while other specialties were established and grew rapidly. Neurosurgery, thoracic surgery, and plastic surgery which had been established in a few centres were quickly provided by the Health Service in every region. Regional radio-therapy services separate from diagnostic radiology were established. The deficiencies in pathology and diagnostic radiology had been exposed by wartime needs and partly remedied, but needed expansion and re-equipment. Anaesthesiology developed rapidly into the largest specialty followed by pathology and psychiatry. The increase in consultants was thus not only in numbers, but much more importantly in range of expertise. Geriatrics and child psychiatry developed from almost nothing; urological and cardiological units were established at least in main centres, pathology became subdivided; orthopaedic surgery became predominantly concerned with repair of trauma and defects at birth or of aging. But rheumatology and rehabilitation were often neglected.

Only a Health Service, the main source of specialist income, could plan for, train, and provide specialist staff in the numbers required to serve the population of every district. The success of such an expansion depended on training. The Spens Committee had recommended essentially a competitive apprenticeship staff structure in the hospital specialties. The senior registrar grade was intended to provide new advanced training posts in all specialties to give progressive experience and responsibility leading to consultant posts. But the establishment was uncontrolled as if the process of natural selection would suffice. All those who failed in the competition for consultant posts, it was assumed, would simply find a place— by implication less worthy—in general practice.

This in retrospect was one of the least wise actions or pieces of inaction in the early 1950s. The control of senior registrars introduced in 1952 was not enough, it took us a decade to realize we must have proper preparation after qualification for any form of medical practice and that general practice needs at least as careful preparation as any hospital specialty. The lessons have not been fully learned even yet and there are still gross injustices to younger doctors whose progress is delayed by the staffing structure of the hospitals rather than their own stage of fitness for responsibility.

Nevertheless through the 1950s the newly regrouped hospitals did provide a district specialist service for the whole population. The concern of the group with the needs of the population of the whole district, once accepted, meant that individual hospitals could not concern themselves only with the needs of patients in or presenting themselves at the hospital on that day. But the logical sequel to that acceptance was not always recognized. The organization of medical work within the hospital was left largely to the individual consultant, and attempts to persuade the profession in the early 1950s to some kind of divisional organization of hospital medical work failed. The antique model of organization of hospital medical staff usual in voluntary teaching hospitals had been generally adopted and insistence upon the clinical independence and equality of all consultants sometimes resulted in failure of co-operation even over such questions as the most efficient use of available operating theatre time. The rapid increase in consultant numbers in itself helped to make the old committee machinery ineffective. Still less was there effective linkage between hospital specialist practice and general practice in the community since consultation over patients, even at domiciliary visits, was infrequent and there was no joint planning machinery.

One of the results of the sharp division between recognized hospital specialist and general practitioner was a serious decline in morale of the general practitioners. This, of course, was exacerbated by the long fight over remuneration. When in 1952 Mr Justice Danckwerts in his adjudication virtually accepted the general practitioners' claim for betterment in their remuneration, they became entitled to a large amount of accumulated back pay. The settlement related total remuneration to the numbers of practitioners and not to population and the needed increase in numbers of general practitioners would not then reduce the average income of those already in practice. The number of Principals increased by about a seventh in the next few years, and some of the increased money (£100 000) available in general practice was by agreement paid annually into a special fund to encourage group practice. It is too seldom recognized that the growth of group practice through the 1950s was the direct result of the decision by the general practitioners to forego £100 000 of the money due to them each year. Some 800 groups were able with this help to provide themselves with new or greatly improved practice premises. The Royal Commission on Medical and Dental Remuneration later pointed out the anomaly in this use of money intended as part of the doctors' income. Thereafter the annual contribution was made from Health Service Funds, until it was superseded by the new system of remuneration known as the general practitioners' charter in 1966 and the Establishment of the General Practice Finance Corporation which now makes loans. From 1948 till 1966 the Health Service used a system of payment in general medical practice which did not even recognize the cost to the individual doctor of providing better premises and it actually penalized the practice which applied a greater than average proportion of gross remuneration to improving the service to patients. This was a relic of the National Health Insurance which neither profession nor government saw to be harmful early enough. The Royal Commission had been set up because of the incessant friction over remuneration. The standing Review Body for medical and dental remuneration it recommended has at least reduced that area of grievance.

While grouping of doctors for mutual support had already begun in a limited way, community nursing had no organized links with individual practices until almost simultaneously in Winchester and Oxford in 1954, arrangements were made to attach a health visitor to a group general practice. This rational development was not generally accepted either by local health authorities or general practitioners until the 1960s, but it was a highly successful demonstration of the advantages of community practice by doctors and nurses working together for the same group of people instead of assigning nurses to areas in each of which many doctors might work.

Not much more than one in six of all general practitioners is in single-handed practice now. The change is much more than the development of partnerships. Well over half the general practitioners are now able to receive the special additional allowance for group practice which was part of the settlement under the general practitioners' charter. Probably three-quarters of all health visitors and general practitioners now work together in a system which is wrongly described as attachment. It is really a doctor/nurse partnership such as occurs naturally in hospital practice. It enables the doctor and nurse to contribute their respective professional skills, complementing each other as they should and facilitating each other's work. It brings us much closer to the concept of family practice as the continuing care of the health of the individual, preferably in the family group, by professionals who are able not merely to respond on request to the medical needs of the individual or the family but also to assume increasingly some of the responsibilities of preventive health work. In some areas the whole of primary care—curative and preventive—is undertaken as part of health centre or group practice.

In some small towns like Frome or Cleckheaton and in some larger centres like Thamesmead or the Cleveland area of Teesside all the doctors work from health centres, not necessarily in partnership with each other, but with health visitors, nurses and midwives and together they provide all the medical and allied services the population of that town or neighbourhood and its neighbouring district need. That sort of situation can be achieved, even if less easily, in large cities and can be established from the beginning in new town developments.

Through the 1950s local health authority services developed in a way that emphasized the absurdity of the fears voiced so loudly by some senior members of the public health sector of the medical profession in 1948. Old style maternity and child welfare work was changing. Emphasis upon medical work in antenatal and infant welfare clinics was slowly diminishing because families had their own doctors, and health visiting developed more selectively with greater emphasis on health education in less didactic form and on the family as a whole. The amount of health visitor time available increased in fifteen years by more than two-fifths, and three-quarters of all infants born in the year attended child health centres at least once in that year. More home nurses were appointed and they, like health visitors, were increasingly concerned with old people at home. The new home help services became one of the most important supporting Health Service developments. Ambulance services were co-ordinated, standardized and expanded and their staffs better trained.

Through the 1950s the proportion of babies born in hospital remained below two-thirds. The birth rate fell until 1954, increased again to a peak in 1964 and thereafter fell until it is now as low as in the early 1930s and still falling. The proportion of babies born in hospital increased, and is now ten-elevenths for the country as a whole. General practitioners have nevertheless played an increased part in midwifery in the home or in the hospital, especially in antenatal care. Indeed the maternity services are now better integrated in hospital and community than most of the rest of the service.

The maternal death rate has fallen by four-fifths during the period of the National Health Service, mainly because of improved antenatal care. The length of stay in hospital after confinement has been falling throughout the period; in 1958 five-sixths of patients stayed more than six days and in 1972 less than half.

In 1948 there were two well-established primary preventive

programmes: immunization against diphtheria has been almost completely successful, smallpox only occurs when infection is imported and is then quickly controlled even though little more than a third of children born between 1948 and 1970 were vaccinated each year. Formerly diphtheria, scarlet fever, poliomyelitis and to a lesser extent, measles and whooping cough were the main reasons for admission to hospitals for infectious diseases. Much of the accommodation in these hospitals was unused by 1948 and many of the beds were therefore used under the Health Service for the treatment of tuberculosis or non-communicable disease, especially for the chronic sick. Where 25 000 beds were set aside at the beginning of the Health Service, fifteen years later less than a fifth of this number were in use for communicable disease. In 1950 the number of cases of pulmonary tuberculosis identified each year was still increasing, but the following year there began a decline which still continues until mortality and incidence are now less than a twentieth of the former level. Economies, the result of these changes, gave the Health Service a large concealed subsidy which was applied to meet other health requirements.

Community mental health services were slowly developed until the Mental Health Act of 1959, have more than doubled since, and have now become the responsibility of the new social welfare departments. Training centres for mentally handicapped children and adults, the former now the responsibility of education authorities and the latter of the social welfare authorities, were among the most important new developments by health authorities during the first twenty years of the Health Service.

It had been possible in the first ten years of the Health Service to realize great improvements by training and recruitment of considerably enlarged staffs, and by a wider deployment of specialized medical and technical staff, but costs had risen far more than anticipated and little had been done about buildings.

The Guillebaud Committee concluded in 1955 that the organization must be given a chance to develop, and that increased costs were not due to bad management but rather to the fact that the original forecasts had had to be made on totally inadequate information. The cost of drugs provided under the Health Service became a constant cause of concern, although that cost *per capita* in fact is lower than the costs in other comparable countries. Repeated attempts to secure economies could not prevent an increase. The reports of first the Hinchcliffe Committee and later the Sainsbury Committee do not really give any grounds for believing that a large reduction in cost is likely. Nor did the efforts of the committee chaired first by Lord Cohen and then by Professor McGregor on the classification of proprietary drugs, lead to much change. There is certainly a great deal less than optimum use of available drugs, but this is sometimes under- rather than over-use. The medical profession itself reviewed the Service from a different point of view and, in 1964, the Porritt report presented the first well-argued case for integration of the three arms of the Service. It is doubtful whether we would have progressed as far without that prompting.

I must turn now to the question of capital investment, particularly in Health Service buildings. The Service inherited a collection of buildings, mostly old, none planned since the 1930s, and all out of date in design. Hospitals lacked modern diagnostic and treatment facilities, particularly operating theatres and laboratories. The wards were mainly of the Nightingale type and nursing facilities in them were sometimes archaic and probably nowhere sufficient. Space and equipment for pathology and radiology were initially insufficient and often obsolete. In such a collection of hospital buildings a great increase in specialized work, particularly of the more complex kinds occurred as staff became available. In twenty-four years admissions increased by nearly two millions. The BMA Annual Meeting in Birmingham in 1957 was perhaps the first occasion for taking a fresh look at what our needs really were. A little later Mr Walpole Lewin and Mr Lawrence Abel wrote a report for the BMA demanding a rate of capital investment in hospitals of £50 million a year. We had spent only £100 million in the first decade of the Health Service mainly in maintenance work, but what capital had been spent on new building had been for operating theatres, laboratories, X-ray departments and out-patient departments. These made it possible to use even bad, old wards with greater efficiency though with heavy demands on staff. In the early 1950s there had been a brief attempt to start a major hospital capital works programme. Something much larger was needed and by husbanding resources a little was found for a small group of larger projects; but the need seemed almost too great for radical solutions to be propounded. Two regions, Oxford and Wessex, attempted a review of what their requirements really were and when the problem was approached as one of re-building with concentration and replacement for efficiency it began to look a little less forbidding. At Mr Enoch Powell's instance all regions were asked to produce plans during 1961 and from these the first hospital building plan for the country was assembled and published in 1962 to be followed a year later by a Health and Welfare Services plan. In the drafting of both those plans Mr Powell played a large personal part.

Though these plans are now out of date and have been substantially revised, their publication was a milestone in the development of both health and social services. They mark the end of the period of patching and making do and the first reasoned attempt to go forward on the national scale required. True the hospital plan was for physical structures but it was based on stated norms which were very different from anything a planner would have put forward in 1948 and had implications for staffing and for functional development especially in the community services. The health and welfare plan was more about developing certain kinds of staff and service than about places to house them. But we had moved on to an attempt to provide the physical resources needed and the plans were to be rolled forward annually and could be timed over a reasonably foreseeable period. Plans of that kind could only work if the professions involved were also revising and reforming their own patterns of training and working.

In 1961 one of the most significant events in the Health Service occurred. Doctors in Exeter and Stoke-on-Trent had formulated ideas for the local development of postgraduate medical education and set out to collect the means to implement them. They wanted to provide themselves locally with meeting places, libraries and the physical facilities needed for continuing education of established doctors and professional training for doctors not yet established. They had quite clear ideas about what they wanted to do but they needed places in which to do it. They were asking at that time simply for the opportunity to put their new buildings on hospital land so that the new centres could be linked with the district general hospitals. Eventually they did get their rent-free sites, but with some support from the Nuffield Provincial Hospitals Trust they collected funds for the buildings largely themselves. That success came later. The idea was taken up by the Nuffield Provincial Hospitals Trust who in December 1961 called a conference at Oxford of a group which included some of the originators of the idea, the Presidents of the Royal Colleges, regional, university and departmental representatives under the chairmanship of Professor Sir George Pickering, Chairman of their Medical Advisory Committee. This group not only agreed on the general principles for what had to be done, but strongly supported maximum voluntary contribution in doing it. The President of the Royal College of Surgeons maintained that every surgeon owed something by way of teaching to surgery; he called it surgical tithing.

Of course there had been local educational activities before that conference, but there had been no general recognition of the need for systematic training on the lines of the residency programmes in North America. Even the pre-registration year was something of a lottery, giving many new graduates not much more than two six-months' apprenticeships.

The Nuffield Provincial Hospitals Trust, when an account of the conference was published, promised substantial financial help and the King Edward's Hospital Fund for London also contributed. The striking response however was local. Some regions, notably Wessex, Oxford and Birmingham, organized programmes for the whole regions. One or two, notably less active, seemed for a time largely unaware of the need for educational activity in every district, but all were eventually involved. In nearly all hospital groups now there are post-graduate educational programmes, teaching accommodation and libraries. Every region has a postgraduate Dean and every group a local tutor. The Nuffield contribution of funds was a crucial bridging operation until in 1964, Exchequer money was committed and the support of future developments assured. But the most significant contribution from the beginning was in the personal effort behind each local project and the readiness of doctors as a whole to contribute funds—an effort that still continues. In many places new, purpose-built centres have been financed wholly by money collected from local benefactors and contributed by the profession itself; such a centre was opened at Poole in August 1973 and fully justified although there was already one at Boscombe only seven miles away. Health Service funds provided through the Regional Hospital Boards have assisted most buildings, provided some wholly and provided maintenance for all. Centrally a Council for Postgraduate Medical Education composed of representatives from universities, the Royal Colleges, and the BMA and financed by the Central Health Departments succeeded an earlier voluntary committee under Sir Robert Aitken set up with funds provided by the Nuffield Provincial Hospitals Trust. The Council first chaired by Professor Robson and now by Sir John Richardson is a unifying and promoting influence in the development of postgraduate education particularly in vocational training which will grow in importance.

The contribution that the new postgraduate centres have already made to the quality of medical care at the periphery is not easily measured. They have had an obvious and important effect in improving communication between general practitioners and hospital staff. If the gap that has existed for over a century between general and specialist practice is ever to be closed, this is the most likely means, and there is no doubt that it must be closed if medicine is to make the progress it should. Moreover there must also be much closer association between the various health professions and better realization of the common ground which must exist in the postgraduate training of them all. Significantly the three centres whose opening I have attended this summer were all multi-disciplinary and associated with training of the other health professions as well.

The worst feature in training and staffing in medicine was the unorganized pattern which failed to provide sensible preparation for general practice or, if a hospital career was the young graduate's objective, led to a needless delay on average of four years beyond the time required before he reached the consultant grade. There is still a serious imbalance between the numbers in training grades and those who are established—especially in the hospitals. It has been made worse by the mistaken reduction in entry to the medical schools during the 1950s, especially after the Willink Report. The intake of two thousand or more foreign graduates a year first helped to conceal the shortage and then to maintain the distorted structure, even though most remain only a limited time.

I shall not discuss undergraduate education save to mention one point—the inadequate academic representation of some vital service components. Chairs in psychiatry were few before 1960 whereas chairs of general practice and geriatrics have appeared only very recently—six in 1973 and largely due to Sir Keith Joseph's help in obtaining voluntary funds.

Parallel to the differentiation of specialties in medical practice there has been a great increase in associated science and technology only now being reorganized on lines recommended in the report of a committee chaired by Lord Zuckerman.

In the first twenty-five years of the National Health Service, a decrease of the order of 10 per cent in the number of hospital beds in use at any one time has occurred. In the same time there was an increase in population of 12 per cent and in the number of patients treated in those beds of the order of 80 per cent. The largest single increase in admissions to general hospitals is for delivery. The other major proportional increases are for the treatment of trauma, for the treatment of patients by some of the most specialized surgical methods and for gynaecology. In psychiatry a remarkable change in the custodial practices of earlier years began about 1954 on a scale sufficient to show itself in the national figures, although of course some pioneers had secured similar results earlier. Between 1954 and 1972 the number of beds actually in use for patients with mental illness in proportion to the population had fallen by a third. The admissions had more than doubled because of a change in pattern of treatment of early mental illness made possible partly by a change in public attitude, partly by professional awareness, and partly by new drugs.

At the same time the number of patients in hospitals for the mentally sub-normal has slightly increased, but this has been due to the longer survival of the severely handicapped in whom infections can be effectively treated, while supportive methods and training at occupational centres have made it possible to keep in the community many more of the less severely handicapped, who would formerly have lived in hospital.

In the care of the chronic sick there has been a radical change in that the number of specialist geriatricians has increased approximately tenfold, and they use much more active methods aimed at rehabilitation and return to the community, in place of the purely custodial attitude of earlier times. I do not suggest that this change has gone nearly far enough, but there are those who do not seem to realize that it has occurred at all, and it is fair to give credit to the pioneers of geriatrics whose example has given hope of recovery at least to a measure of independence for many old people who would formerly have lived out a meagre, inactive existence in a hospital ward. Indeed their very success has increased the load as it leaves them with older and more frail patients to treat.

There has thus been change in hospital work leading to shortened stay of patients, whether it be after delivery, investigation, abdominal surgery or treatment for a stroke or pulmonary tuberculosis. Greatly increased sub-division of specialties has occurred among the medical staff so that there are now twice as many specialties listed as in 1949. Inevitably this requires greater reliance upon community services especially general medical practice, both for pre-hospital care and after-care of patients who have been retained in hospital for a shorter time. Out-patient references have increased by about one-fifth in proportion to population but this is largely explained by the increase in accidents and the services their victims require, the recognition of the value of out-patient services in psychiatry and geriatrics and their consequent increased use, and the very necessary increase in antenatal care. The number of patients seeking care at accident and emergency departments has increased in a way that suggests some need for better arrangements in general practice for immediate help in minor incidents. The amount of investigation has been greatly increased and diagnostic services in pathology and radiology and to some extent cardiology have been made available direct to general practitioners whose share of the work of the pathology and radiology departments has gone up by half to an eighth of the total. All told, the amount of medical work required in hospital must have been at least doubled and the amount of scientific and technological support for it has been increased even more, since scientific and technical staff have been increased by two and a half times, and the potential for service by much more, using the new methods and equipment now available.

The scientific sophistication of hospital medical practice involved in the care of the individual patient is far more than twenty-five years ago. The separation of the service in a hospital into so many specialties makes those specialties not more independent in their work but ever more dependent upon each other. It follows that specialist work must be organized and this need, which has only been perceived within the last few years, is now beginning to be met in most of our larger general hospitals, though as yet in primitive form. To quote from a recent World Health Organization report 'the change in resource allocation and structure of the health service is unlikely to be effective by itself. Management of the system at all levels is essential, and it is felt that such management can be meaningful and effective, and at the same time be simple.' That the complex, very expensive resources of the hospital need such medical organization is obvious to others concerned with hospital services, and it is inevitable that there will be management intervention from outside to cure inefficiency if the health professions do not provide it themselves. The Platt Working Party on hospital medical staff in 1960 asked only for adoption of the simple firm system common in the old voluntary hospitals. That is better than nothing, but it is insufficient except within a general pattern such as the divisional system recommended by the Cogwheel Working Party only six years later. The hospital part of the service has hardly begun to reap the benefits that are attainable from better management of what we have, and still less has the service as a whole. Of course we have not enough, but mere addition of resources to those inefficiently used will not suffice. At the time that the Platt Working Party was deliberating, the concept of district organization around a district general hospital had not been fully accepted. Now every district has at least the beginnings of its future general hospital, and some complete new district general hospitals are already in use. At least in every district people now know where they are trying to go. There may have been some mistakes in planning—probably nowhere more apparent than in Greater London—and there are places where unforeseen population movements made modification of earlier plans necessary but, broadly, plans for hospital and community service development, adjusted to the geography and demography of the country, do exist.

There still remain serious weaknesses in the links between hospital and general medical practice, between hospital and home nursing and between health service and personal social services. Movement towards group practice, association of community nursing staff with general practice, better links between hospital and home care, and an educational focus at the postgraduate centres (preferably for all the health professionals) give the opportunity of improvement. The changes in general practice will make that easier and the involvement of general practitioners in the divisional organization of hospital medical work would ensure recognition of the fact that the treatment of hospital in-patients and the investigation of out-patients can only be fully effective if hospital medical staff rely upon the resources of general practice for pre- and post-hospital care.

In the last seven years the medical profession has come to accept that the Service should provide premises for general practice. In the first fifteen years of the Health Service, only seventeen new health services were opened in England. In the following seven years, four hundred were opened, over a hundred of them last year in England and Wales. There are almost another four hundred in the pipeline in England and Wales, more than we have resources to build. There are between seven and eight hundred general practices in group premises provided by doctors themselves. In Teesside it is possible to foresee that all general practices and all the community nurses will be working from health centres or their equivalent before 1980, and other areas, both urban and rural, may do as well.

Personal preventive services provided by local health authorities have changed. Some social services, fostered in health departments, have been transferred from health departments to social service departments—rightly, because they depend more upon social work than upon medicine itself. Nonetheless, health services must retain a working interface with social welfare. The need for preventive medical work remains, but the method of its organization has changed and is still changing. The primary preventive services of immunization have been the most successfully organized. Medical Officers of Health have been able to involve general practitioners in their provision especially in services working on a computer programme.

There are however rapidly developing new fields for preventive medicine. First, there is an area in which the major activity is central. Potent drugs inevitably have dangers and the control of the introduction and surveillance of adverse effects of drugs, must be undertaken centrally by an expert group with appropriate, professionally trained, expert staff. A central system of monitoring adverse reactions must continue. Some of the problems of chemicals in the environment require central investigation, for instance mercury or lead content of foods, or the effects of more complex chemicals such as pesticides, curing agents or food additives, but the preventive action and control activity often have to be local, for instance to detect and restrict the discharge of lead containing dust from an industrial undertaking or excessive exposure of workers.

The question of admissibility of food additives or the use of substances like cyclamates, saccharine or brominated vegetable oils could only be handled centrally. Yet epidemiological surveillance of local sources of toxic substances may have to be undertaken partly by experts concerned with industrial resources, and partly by those concerned locally with community health.

Prevention in a secondary sense is likely to be attempted by using new methods for the detection of pre-symptomatic disease. Screening in an organized health service can be used selectively by family doctors but will need to be promoted by the community physician concerned with the health of the community as a whole rather than of each individual. Screening for some congenital abnormalities is well established and commonly undertaken by non-medical staff, but more complex methods involving amniocentesis for detection of chromosome or metabolic anomalies are now being studied. The community's requirement for services of various kinds and the effectiveness of the services need assessment and presentation to the clinicians involved in providing the services. How, for instance, can we know about the real outcome of myocardial infarction without following up the results of each episode as a whole? A community physician's function is not the monitoring of the treatment of individual patients but he is needed to collate information about results in the population and to present it in a form which it can be effectively used by clinical colleagues in hospital and general practice. Sir Richard Doll has analysed the advantages to be gained and the pitfalls to be avoided in his recent Nuffield Lecture.*

The supporting services in the community must be organized, including co-ordination with community nursing and social services. Advice will be required by the education and social welfare departments of the local authority on the health implications of some of the services they provide. The education authority will need someone versed in the medical aspects of special educational requirements for the handicapped child. The quantity and variety of services needed by both his colleagues and the community of the future leave no doubt of the need for a community physician. The range is so wide that some doubt whether there are doctors sufficiently prepared for the responsibility. The London School of Hygiene and Tropical Medicine has pioneered in England training with the requisite range. The medical profession has accepted that this is a specialty like any other and worthy of similar rewards. The Hunter Working Party has amply presented the case. True there are dissenting 'noises off' in otherwise enlightened quarters, but to me it would be as silly to try to dispense with

* *Proc. Roy. Soc. Med.*, August 1973.

this co-ordinating and investigative function as to try to run a medical school without a Dean.

I have not discussed dentistry, pharmacy or the ophthalmic services, great as their contribution has been and will be, because I have too little time. I will only make the obvious point that they are essential parts of a comprehensive service and I only omit further reference because I cannot do them justice.

I have tried to show how the three main components in the present system of medical care have advanced in the first twenty-five years to the point where they now are and where there must be a change in the administrative supporting structure. I have not attempted to discuss that structure beyond saying that it will be revised. The Regional and Area Health Authorities now exist and the District Management Teams must soon be established. The logic of the new system is clear with regional overall planning and management in districts under area authorities which are to work closely with the relevant local authorities for the same area. There will be a management component which can assist professional and technical developments to go forward more rapidly on lines which are already established. There will be professional participation in management, but it should not be dominant at the expense of public involvement. There will be no clinical interference but there is of course the opportunity of channelling financial and other resources in particular ways which could affect the relative emphasis given to different parts of the Service. That is a possibility that makes medical and other professional advisory machinery essential to prevent distortion of professional services by some arbitrary management process. It should also allow the formulation of better informed professional conclusions about what it is best to do with the resources we have.

The management principles are well known, but there remains a real problem of ensuring that appointed managing bodies are sufficiently responsive to local needs and views. The Community Health Councils are the new and untried element which must be made to work if public confidence is to be maintained. These councils, consisting of local people interested in the Health Service and with access to it and to information about its working, can become invaluable means of ensuring public support. If they are mishandled and antagonized they will certainly become pressure groups for those with real or imagined grievances against the Health Service and constant irritants to the management. Health authorities will need to make a real effort to help them.

Medical research has made great advances for reasons not intrinsic to the Service, but the Service has benefited greatly in the last decade from the rapid expansion—about forty-fold—of support of decentralized research from Health Service funds. The amount now spent by the Department of Health and Social Security is ten times this and Dr R. H. L. Cohen, who fostered this growth, is one of the unsung heroes of the Health Service.

No-one can really imagine that every conceivable demand for health service can be met. There will have to be some consideration of priorities.

Look at the last twenty-five years. The greatest priority tends to have been given to areas of greatest scientific interest. New developments like kidney transplantation, cardiac surgery, super-voltage radiotherapy and intermittent haemodialysis attracted large shares of development resources for reasons that may not seem adequate to all members of either the public or the professions when it is known that the mere amenities of life in some aspects of the Health Service, mainly those concerned with long-term care and with patients who cannot assert themselves, have been so lacking as to be unacceptable by any standards of normal living.

The plain fact is that too few people either of the public or the professions have had real contact with conditions in long stay hospitals which have often been the worst of our hospital structures, the least inviting for the patients and staff alike. The sensitivity of some but not of all the patients may have been diminished. The demands upon staff looking after these groups of patients may give the least obvious reward in terms of an effective result from their efforts. The shortcomings are there for all to see—that is all who go to look and that number is not large. Conditions are easily presented as scandalous, and in terms of the amenities of modern life they often are so. It is a poor salve to our consciences to say that the patients concerned may themselves be less aware of the shortcomings than we who see them. We have small ground for saying that, when we do not ourselves suffer them literally for years on end as many patients do.

In the limited total availability of resources, we may have to make arbitrary decisions that this or that highly expensive form of therapy, of great scientific interest, with uncertain outcome for the individual patient, must wait while we make good the obvious deficiencies of care available to this long-stay group. If we do make decisions of that kind we must be careful that we do not delay the progress of more intensively applied medicine which could benefit many. We might, for instance, through earlier, intensive rehabilitation of the patient who has suffered a stroke, prevent him from becoming one of the long-stay chronic sick, to his advantage and the economic advantage of the service. The decisions are not usually of that kind. The demand for very expensive therapies tends naturally to be for the very few. We need careful judgement as to how far each is justifiable, bearing in mind that it may lead on to a much wider application, through the development of medical science, for the benefit of many rather than the uncertain progress of the few. For instance, pioneer work on transplantation of organs at relatively high cost in professional and scientific effort is justified if it leads us to efficient systems of renal transplantation such as that evolved in Denmark. The alternative may be that a larger number of patients must be kept on intermittent dialysis at even greater cost in professional time and funds. Transplantation also contributes scientific information in the field of immunology which may eventually contribute to better treatment of malignant disease or other chronic diseases which put heavy loads on the Health Service. The same arguments cannot at present be adduced for heart transplants, but they might be for coronary by-pass surgery.

We should not try to arrest medical scientific progress at, say, the 1974 level in order to attempt to perfect the situation for all. If we do, the drive will go out of medicine and medical science and the outcome will be to the disadvantage of all patients. But equally we must not press blindly ahead in science without making such provision as is practicable for the common things which most commonly occur in medicine. Research is useless without development. We must not forget that of the 380 000 or so hospital beds which are occupied at this moment in England and Wales, five out of eight are occupied by patients who are mentally ill, mentally handicapped or chronic sick. These are the expensive patients in our hospitals because though only 10 per cent of in-patients in a year they stay so long: Society cannot accept for them a grossly defective standard of care. It must do what is possible and be cognisant of what that is. It is unmindfulness which we must combat. Nor can we disregard the needs of the very much larger number of frail, handicapped, even bedridden old peoole who are at home with community support which may be much too small.

I must also point out that we have allowed gross disparities in resources between different regions with only partial correction during twenty-five years. Indeed the widest disparity—that between expenditure on the hospital services in Scotland compared with England and Wales—has increased materially in the last decade so that *per capita* expenditure is now 25 per cent greater in Scotland. Even Wales spends £1 *per capita* more than England on Health and Social Services.

The realization of the district concept of health services organization will give us a complex in every district of comprehensive general hospital, health centres or group practices, and as the focal point the postgraduate institute, all of which should be maintained by the greater medical profession, not by doctors alone. There are forces within the professions already producing the elements of this pattern. The future of the Health Service must be to ensure that those elements do in fact bring together the other health professions with medicine, and the many components of medicine itself. Management must support this and ensure the proper deployment of resources without seeking to direct clinical management or procedures. The health professions and sciences share with management the overall responsibility for securing the best results we can achieve. The outcome will not be perfect and if any of us ever thinks it is at some future time, then that one has outlived his usefulness to the Service. There will always be more that can be done. But the result that we achieve must be the best that the resources available to us permit in both technical and human terms. We are only at the beginning of the rational organization of professional work and as we go on some of the most cherished illusions about the rights, duties and responsibilities of individual professions or specialties, may come in question. There is inertia in the professions that even rejects the asking of questions. We must overcome that. There is nothing against our asking questions about the most fundamental assumptions involved in the Health Service so long as the questioner does not assume the answer before he asks—as some do.

I am not a chauvinist about the Health Service. I do not believe it is uniquely perfect with nothing to learn of the different methods and experiences of other countries. We know that some things are better done in some places in other countries. Bluntly, they can show better results which we cannot explain away. I think we should make far more use of the increasing opportunities for exchange of information with them. I believe that the World Health Organization will, in the years to come, have much to teach us all about this. But I do believe that at this time I would be as safe seeking treatment at random in this country as in any country in the world. If I were lucky in my choice in another country I might do better. If I were unlucky I might do a great deal worse. I just think that the element of luck enters into it less in Britain than elsewhere.